Zaner-Bloser

Handwriting

Practice Masters

5

W9-AAZ-098

Copyright © Zaner-Bloser, Inc.   ISBN 0-7367-1231-3

The pages in this book may be duplicated for classroom use. Zaner-Bloser, Inc.

Zaner-Bloser, Inc., P.O. Box 16764,
Columbus, Ohio 43216-6764

1-800-421-3018

Printed in the United States of America

02 03 04 05 06 (106) 5 4 3 2 1

Contents

Practice Masters

Support Materials

Name:

Write the letter and the joinings.

i i i i i i i

i i i i i i i

is   ia   ig   im   in

Write the words and the sentences.

immense   imperial   incident

inferior   income   inland

inhabit   inform   inquire

This is my sister Tina.

She is six.

Name:

Write the letter and the joinings.

t t t t t t t

t t t t t t t

th tr ta to ty

Write the words and the sentences.

tart teenager teaspoon

taunt termite thicket

timber tissue tractor

Matt beat me at tennis.

It was interesting.

Name:

● Write the letter and the joinings.

uu *uu* *uu* *uu* *uu* *uu* *uu*

uu *uu* *uu* *uu* *uu* *uu* *uu*

ur *us* *ua* *ud* *un*

Write the words and the sentences.

unaware *urgent* *guard*

● *studio* *tuxedo* *umpire*

house *hiccup* *mule*

A quart measures volume.

I studied until four.

●

Practice Master 3

Name:

Write the letter and the joinings.

w   *w*   *w*   *w*   *w*   *w*

w   *w*   *w*   *w*   *w*   *w*

we   *wr*   *wo*   *wa*   *wy*

Write the words and the sentences.

waltz   *ward*   *weasel*

whew   *wick*   *wrung*

growl   *snowy*   *wool*

She watched out the window.

What will the weather be like?

Name: _____

Write the letter and the joinings.

e   e   e   e   e   e   e   e

e   e   e   e   e   e   e

el   ei   ea   en   em

Write the words and the sentences.

ease   elegant   seedling

●

eggshell   either   empire

enable   editor   money

Did you remember your essay?

Everyone is ready to eat.

●

Practice Master 5

Name:

Write the letter and the joinings.

l   l   l   l   l   l

l   l   l   l   l   l

le   ll   la   lo   ly

Write the words and the sentences.

labor   lecture   jelly

lonely   palm   talcum

fault   ulna   lollipop

Pull the lever on the left.

The candle still flickered.

Practice Master 6

Name: _____

Write the letter and the joinings.

_b_ _b_ _b_ _b_ _b_ _b_ _b_

_b_ _b_ _b_ _b_ _b_ _b_ _b_

_bu_ _bb_ _bo_ _ba_ _by_

Write the words and the sentences.

bachelor _boost_ _hobby_

blank _husband_ _beehive_

bind _barbecue_ _bracelet_

The baby broke the bottle.

Boiling water makes it bubble.

Practice Master 7

Name:

Write the letter and the joinings.

h   h   h   h   h   h   h   h

h   h   h   h   h   h   h

he   ht   ho   ha   hy

Write the words and the sentences.

height   homeland   hammock

filthy   history   heavy

handbag   shovel   bright

I had a hunch about her.

She is a happy child.

Name: _____

Write the letter and the joinings.

f   f   f   f   f   f   f

f   f   f   f   f   f   f

fe   ff   fa   fo   fy

Write the words and the sentences.

ferret   family   taffy

flourish   fluffy   forfeit

friend   fever   favorite

The waffles were eaten fast.

My favorite food is french fries.

Practice Master 9

Name:

Write the letter and the joinings.

k   k   k   k   k   k   k

k   k   k   k   k   k   k

ke   kl   ko   kn   ky

Write the words and the sentences.

kernel   backache   lucky

cockroach   knuckle   kimono

hickory   kindle   bankrupt

The kettle was knocked over.

The kids wore knickers.

Practice Master 10

Name: _____

Write the letter and the joinings.

_r_ _r_ _r_ _r_ _r_ _r_ _r_ _r_

_r_ _r_ _r_ _r_ _r_ _r_ _r_

_ru_ _rr_ _rd_ _rc_ _rn_

Write the words and the sentences.

backyard   mercy   forlorn

furry   reverse   sharp

scrape   marvel   normal

The red raspberries are tart.

The river was too rough to raft.

Practice Master II

Name:

Write the letter and the joinings.

s   s   s   s   s   s   s

s   s   s   s   s   s   s

sh   st   sc   sn   sy

Write the words and the sentences.

shiver   crust   escape

esquire   severe   sanity

solvent   spasm   glossy

The scrapbook was messy.

The solution is simple.

Practice Master 12   Copyright © Zaner-Bloser, Inc.

Name:

Write the letter and the joinings.

j   j   j   j   j   j   j

j   j   j   j   j   j   j

je   ju   ji   ja   jo

Write the words and the sentences.

juniper   jut   jolt

jealous   adjoin   jitters

jockey   jeans   jungle

The jacket just fit.

We judged the jump rope contest.

Name:

Write the letter and the joinings.

p   p   p   p   p   p   p

p   p   p   p   p   p   p

pr   pl   po   pa   py

Write the words and the sentences.

plume   polar   patriot

pneumonia   penguin   phase

canopy   proud   pumpkin

Please pass the popcorn.

The puppy is so playful.

Name:

• Write the letter and the joinings.

a   a   a   a   a   a   a

a   a   a   a   a   a   a

ar   as   ag   ac   an

Write the words and the sentences.

arena   achieve   birthday

• answer   atlas   amble

aardvark   acquaint   aluminum

The atlas has pages of maps.

Carry the crafts with care.

•

Practice Master 15

Name:

Write the letter and the joinings.

d   *d*   *d*   *d*   *d*   *d*   *d*

d   *d*   *d*   *d*   *d*   *d*   *d*

de   *dr*   *dw*   *da*   *do*

Write the words and the sentences.

dapple   *debate*   *draft*

dwell   *moldy*   *doughnut*

ready   *dismiss*   *dust*

The student's desk was dusty.

There are daffodils in the meadow.

Name: _____

g   g   g   g   g   g   g

g   g   g   g   g   g   g

gr   ge   ga   gn   gy

Write the words and the sentences.

gravity   govern   gander

● gnat   might   suggest

again   align   energy

The right glove was gold.

That jagged edge is dangerous.

●

Practice Master 17

Name:

Write the letter and the joinings.

o   *o*   *o*   *o*   *o*   *o*   *o*

o   *o*   *o*   *o*   *o*   *o*   *o*

ou   *op*   *oa*   *oo*   *ov*

Write the words and the sentences.

outlet   *operate*   *board*

noodle   *boxer*   *shovel*

solve   *knock*   *random*

Scott offered an apology.

The scooter was lost.

Name: _____

● Write the letter and the joinings.

_c___c___c___c___c___c___c_

_c___c___c___c___c___c___c_

_cl___ci___ca___co___cy_

Write the words and the sentences.

_classic_____calendar_____collapse_

● _cymbal_____eczema_____cruise_

_success_____carriage_____democracy_

The record was scratched.

We crossed a crystal clear creek.

●

Practice Master 19

Name: _____

Write the letter and the joinings.

_q_ _q_ _q_ _q_ _q_ _q_

_q_ _q_ _q_ _q_ _q_ _q_

_qu_ _qu_ _qu_ _aqu_ _squ_

Write the words and the sentences.

quaint   _quake_   _qualify_

quality   _quarry_   _quill_

question   _squint_   _squirrel_

I qualified for the quarterfinals.

The quiz had seven questions.

Write the letter and the joinings.

n n n n n n n

n n n n n n n

ne   ni   nd   ny   nn

Write the words and the sentences.

newborn   nickel   harmony

sunny   blanket   dense

napkin   singer   frenzy

The nervous bunny ran away.

Our oven was never turned on.

Practice Master 21

Name:

Write the letter and the joinings.

m m m m m m m

m m m m m m m m

me mb mo ma mm

Write the words and the sentences.

measles number macaroni

summer smile bumper

maintain autumn mystery

My memory fails me.

I might remember the poem.

Practice Master 22

Name:

Write the letter and the joinings.

y   *y*   *y*   *y*   *y*   *y*   *y*

y   *y*   *y*   *y*   *y*   *y*   *y*

yi   *ys*   *ya*   *yo*   *ym*   *yn*

Write the words and the sentences.

mystery   *youngster*   *dynamite*

yellow   *yonder*   *symbol*

symptom   *yeast*   *cylinder*

This book is a mystery.

The stray puppy was sleepy.

Practice Master 23

Name: _____

Write the letter and the joinings.

x   x   x   x   x   x   x

x   x   x   x   x   x   x

xe   xp   xc   xa   xy

Write the words and the sentences.

boxer   expect   excited

examine   mixture   exercise

oxygen   peroxide   exact

A hexagon has six sides.

The next textbook is mine.

Practice Master 24

Name:

Write the letter and the joinings.

v   *v*   *v*   *v*   *v*   *v*   *v*

v   *v*   *v*   *v*   *v*   *v*   *v*

ve   *vi*   *vo*   *va*   *vy*

Write the words and the sentences.

venture   *volume*   *vacuum*

gravy   *vehicle*   *viewer*

voyage   *variety*   *revved*

The velvet vest is expensive.

I was nervous to travel.

Practice Master 25

Name:

Write the letter and the joinings.

Z Z Z Z Z Z Z

Z Z Z Z Z Z Z

ze   za   zo   zy   zz

Write the words and the sentences.

magazine   zero   ozone

zoom   muzzle   zipper

guzzle   hazy   memorize

A dozen citizens were in the plaza.

We had frozen pizza for dinner.

Name: _____

Read the menu to answer the questions below.

Tuna Melt $1.98		**Milk Shake** $2.00
Hamburger $2.50		**Fruit Juice** $1.00
Turkey Sandwich $3.47		**Cheese** $0.25
Popcorn $0.99		**Pickles** $0.10
Onion Rings $1.56		**Water** . . . . free

1. How much is a turkey sandwich and onion rings?

_____

_____

2. How much is a tuna melt and a milk shake?

_____

_____

3. How much is a hamburger with cheese and pickles, plus a water?

_____

_____

4. How much is popcorn and fruit juice?

_____

_____

5. How much is a tuna melt with pickles, and fruit juice?

_____

_____

6. How much money will you save if you order water instead of a milk shake?

_____

_____

Name: _____

Below is a list of the number of days Mr. Ramsey's students attended class. Answer the questions below.

Adams, Greg	187 days
Barrett, Tonya	149 days
Donaldson, Simon	165 days
Franks, Kimi	182 days
Groenig, Henry	173 days
Jeras, Josie	179 days

1. How many days did Henry attend school?

_____

_____

2. How many days did Josie attend school?

_____

_____

3. How many days did Simon attend school?

_____

_____

4. How many days did the student with the highest attendance attend?

_____

_____

6. How many days did the student with the lowest attendance attend?

_____

_____

Write the letter, joinings, and words.

A A A A A A A

Af   Al   Aa   Ad   An

Arizona   Alaska   Alabama

Arkansas   Austria   Argentina

Africa   Angola   Antarctica

Albania   Algeria   Andorra

Are we going to visit Ashley?

Apples are the main ingredient.

Practice Master 29

Name: _____

Write the letter, words, and sentences.

O O O O O O O

New Orleans   Oscar Wilde

Ohio   Oklahoma   Ontario

Oceania   Oahu   Odessa

Oneida   Omaha   Ottawa

Oxford   Ozark   Oswego

Omar hiked the Ozark Mountains.

Oh no! I forgot!

Name:

Write the letter, words, and sentences.

D D D D D D D

Dorothea Dix   Frederick Douglass

Delaware   Dalton   Dominica

Dallas   Denmark   Detroit

Durham   Durango   Dublin

Davenport   Dresden   Decatur

Do you know the directions?

Drive carefully.

Practice Master 31

Name: _____

Write the letter, joinings, and words.

C   C   C   C   C   C   C

Cr   Ce   Ca   Co   Cy

California   Cambodia   Canada

Colorado   Croatia   Connecticut

Cyprus   Cadiz   Cairo

Camden   Cambridge   Carthage

Can you call me back?

We took a trip to Cape Canaveral.

Name: _____

Write the letter, joinings, and words.

E   *E*   *E*   *E*   *E*   *E*   *E*

Es   *Er*   *Eo*   *Ea*   *Ey*

Ecuador   *England*   *Estonia*

Ethiopia   *Evansville*   *Eureka*

Edgewood   *Edmonton*   *Edinburg*

Elkton   *Elkhart*   *Eastport*

Everyone arrived on time.

Each flower bloomed this week.

Practice Master 33

Name: _____

Write the letter, joinings, and words.

n n n n n n n

Nu Ne Na No Ny

North Dakota Norway Norman

New York New Jersey Norwalk

New Mexico Nigeria Netherlands

North Carolina Nevada Nebraska

Nobody is home.

Next week is vacation.

Practice Master 34

Name: _____

Write the letter, joinings, and words.

M M M M M M M

Mi   Me   Ma   Mo   My

Massachusetts Monaco Maryland

Macedonia   Missouri   Mexico

Minnesota   Maine   Manchester

Mississippi   Montana   Magnolia

Mr. Martin is our neighbor.

My mother works at the mall.

Name:

Write the letter, joinings, and words.

H H H H H H H

He Hi Hu Ho Ha

Hawaii Hong Kong Highland

Honduras Hungary Hillsboro

Hampton Hammond Henderson

Hartford Houston Holland

Have you been to Hong Kong?

He is my best friend.

Practice Master 36

Name:

Write the letter, joinings, and words.

K   K   K   K   K   K   K

Ke   Kl   Ko   Kn   Ky

Kansas   Kuwait   Kingsport

Key West   Keene   Kenya

Killarney   Kodiak   Kiowa

Kirkwood   Kingston   Knoxville

Keep your receipt.

Knowing your address is useful.

Practice Master 37

Name: _____

Write the letter, joinings, and words.

U U U U U U U

Ul Up Ua Ud Un

Uganda Ukraine Utah

Urbana Utica Uman

Upton Utopia Ulm

Underwood Ulan Ulster

Until now, I was confused.

Uncle Sam represents the U.S.A.

Write the letter, joinings, and words.

Y   Y   Y   Y   Y   Y   Y

Ye   Yu   Yi   Ya   Yo

Yugoslavia   Yukon   Yacuma

Yola   York   New York

Yellowstone   Yaco   Yeso

Yemen   Yungay   Youngsville

You are my friend.

Yesterday was Tuesday.

Practice Master 39

Name:

Write the letter, joinings, and words.

Z   Z   Z   Z   Z   Z   Z

Zw   Zi   Zo   Za   Zy

Zambia   Zimbabwe   Zachary

Zamora   Zanesville   Zorgo

Zapata   Zara   Zadar

New Zealand   Zaragoza   Zalau

Zach took us to the zoo.

The San Diego Zoo was fun.

Practice Master 40

Name:

Write the letter, words, and sentences.

V V V V V V V V

Valley Forge   *Valentine's Day*

Virginia   *Venezuela*   *Victoria*

Vermont   *Vancouver*   *Venice*

Vail   *Valentine*   *Vanderbilt*

Vega   *Las Vegas*   *Vienna*

Valet parking is convenient.

Venus is a planet.

Practice Master 41

Name:

Write the letter, words, and sentences.

W W W W W W W

The Civil War   War of 1812

Washington   Wisconsin   Welch

Wyoming   Wabasco   Wakefield

Waldron   Wellington   Weston

West Virginia   Wales   Westminster

Why don't we rest now?

Webster was worried.

Name:

Write the letter, words, and sentences.

X   X   X   X   X   X   X

Xanadu   Xerxes

Xau   Xibu   Xenia

Xaxim   Xavier   Xinba

Xanthi   Xixian   Xinshi

Xiaoxi   Xativa   Xam

Sign your name at the X.

X marks the spot.

Practice Master 43

Name: _____

Write the letter, words, and sentences.

I I I I I I I

Independence Day   Isaac Newton

Idaho   Indiana   Iowa

Indonesia   Ireland   Italy

Irving   Indianapolis   Iberia

Illinois   Iceland   Irondale

I am writing an essay.

It is due tomorrow.

Name: _____

Write the letter, words, and sentences.

J J J J J J J

Je   Ju   Ji   Jo   Ja

Jamaica   Jordan   Jasper

Jacksonville   Joliet   Jenkins

Johnson   Junction   Juneau

Jarratt   Jewett   Jenkins

Just remember to call me.

Justice is served.

Practice Master 45

Name:

Write the letter, words, and sentences.

Q Q Q Q Q Q Q

John Quincy Adams   Queen Anne

Quebec   Quiltman   Quincy

Queenstown   Quartz   Quatar

Quintin   Quinter   Quesada

Quimby   Quinto   Quetta

Quails are beautiful birds.

Quickly close the door.

Name: _____

Write the letter, words, and sentences.

T T T T T T T T T

Theodore Roosevelt   Harry Truman

Taiwan   Tanzania   Tennessee

Turkey   Texas   Tacoma

Taylor   Tecumseh   Tulsa

Tempe   Torrance   Trinidad

Tryouts are Tuesday.

Thank you very much.

Practice Master 47

Name: _____

Write the letter, words, and sentences.

F   *F*   *F*   *F*   *F*   *F*   *F*   *F*

Ben Franklin   *Francis Scott Key*

Finland   *Florida*   *Fairbanks*

Fairfax   *Fairmont*   *Falmouth*

Fayette   *Farmington*   *Ferguson*

Fisher   *Franklin*   *Florence*

Flutes are great instruments.

Follow the directions closely.

Name:

Write the letter, words, and sentences.

G G G G G G G G

General Grant   Golden Gate Bridge

Georgia   Gambia   Germany

Greece   Guinea   Glenwood

Galveston   Garland   Glasgow

Genoa   Guadeloupe   Gary

Glasses help you see better.

Guess who's here.

Name: _____

Write the letter, words, and sentences.

S   *S*   *S*   *S*   *S*   *S*   *S*

South Beach   St. Petersburg

Scotland   Singapore   Somalia

Sweden   Switzerland   Sussex

Sicily   Seymour   Southport

Seneca   Sycamore   Sterling

Should we turn in our homework?

I attend Stanford University.

Name:

L   L   L   L   L   L   L

Abraham Lincoln   Lake Huron

Louisiana   Latvia   Lebanon

Liberia   Lithuania   Las Vegas

Linden   Lowell   Lisbon

Lockport   Lincoln   Laos

Last week was stormy.

Let me get your coat.

Practice Master 51

Name: _____

Write the letter, words, and sentences.

P P P P P P P

Penn Station   Paul Revere

Pennsylvania   Paris   Poland

Panama   Paraguay   Portugal

Pedro   Parma   Portland

Peru   Pembroke   Pomeroy

Please pass the pepper.

Pepper makes me sneeze.

Write the letter, joinings, and words.

R R R R R R R

Ra Re Ri Ro Ry

Romania Rwanda Roanoke

Randolph Rochester Regina

Rockwell Riverside Redmond

Ronald Reagan Betsy Ross

Remember to wash your hands.

Rest your tired feet.

Practice Master 53

Name:

Write the letter and the words.

B B B B B B B

Benjamin Harrison   Beverly Cleary

Bahamas   Barbados   Bermuda

Bolivia   Brazil   Belize

Berwick   Brooklyn   Boise

Blanco   Bryson   Brewster

Be nice to your brother.

Blow out the candles!

Record of Student's Handwriting Skills

Cursive

	Needs Improvement	Shows Mastery		Needs Improvement	Shows Mastery
Sits correctly	☐	☐	Writes the undercurve to undercurve joining	☐	☐
Positions paper correctly	☐	☐	Writes the undercurve to downcurve joining	☐	☐
Holds pencil correctly	☐	☐	Writes the undercurve to overcurve joining	☐	☐
Writes undercurve strokes	☐	☐	Writes the checkstroke to undercurve joining	☐	☐
Writes downcurve strokes	☐	☐	Writes the checkstroke to downcurve joining	☐	☐
Writes overcurve strokes	☐	☐	Writes the checkstroke to overcurve joining	☐	☐
Writes slant strokes	☐	☐	Writes the overcurve to undercurve joining	☐	☐
Writes i, t, u, w	☐	☐	Writes the overcurve to downcurve joining	☐	☐
Writes e, l, b, h, f, k	☐	☐	Writes the overcurve to overcurve joining	☐	☐
Writes r, s, j, p	☐	☐	Writes with correct shape	☐	☐
Writes a, d, g, o, c, q	☐	☐	Writes with correct size	☐	☐
Writes n, m, y, x, v, z	☐	☐	Writes with correct spacing	☐	☐
Writes numerals 1–10	☐	☐	Writes with correct slant	☐	☐
Writes A, O, D, C, E	☐	☐	Regularly checks written work for legibility	☐	☐
Writes N, M, H, K	☐	☐			
Writes U, Y, Z	☐	☐			
Writes V, W, X	☐	☐			
Writes I, J, Q	☐	☐			
Writes T, F	☐	☐			
Writes G, S, L	☐	☐			
Writes P, R, B	☐	☐			

Manuscript Alphabet

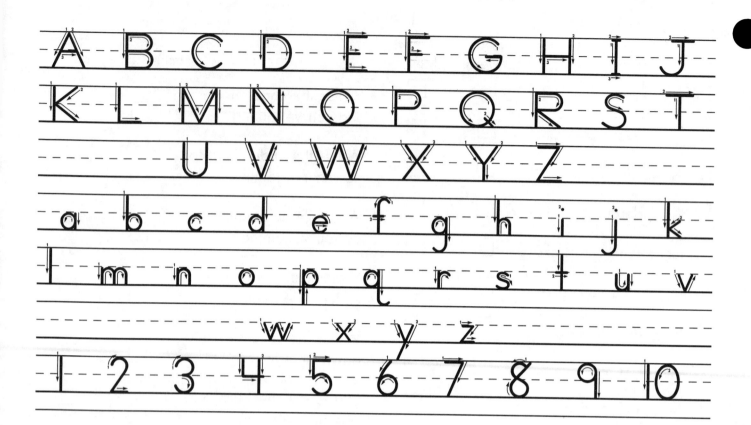

Cursive Alphabet

Cursive Stroke Descriptions

Undercurve.
Slant; undercurve (lift).
Dot.

Undercurve.
Slant; undercurve (lift).
Slide right.

Undercurve.
Slant; undercurve.
Slant; undercurve.

Undercurve.
Slant; undercurve.
Slant; undercurve.
Checkstroke.

Undercurve; loop back; slant;
undercurve.

Undercurve; loop back; slant;
undercurve.

Undercurve; loop back; slant;
undercurve.
Checkstroke.

Undercurve; loop back; slant.
Overcurve; slant; undercurve.

Undercurve; loop back; slant;
loop forward.
Undercurve.

Undercurve; loop back; slant.
Overcurve; curve forward;
curve under.
Slant right; undercurve.

Undercurve.
Slant right.
Slant; undercurve.

Undercurve.
Retrace; curve down and back.
Undercurve.

Undercurve.
Slant; loop back; overcurve
(lift).
Dot.

Undercurve.
Slant; loop back; overcurve;
curve back.
Undercurve.

Downcurve; undercurve.
Slant; undercurve.

Downcurve; undercurve.
Slant; undercurve.

Downcurve; undercurve.
Slant; loop back; overcurve.

Downcurve; undercurve.
Checkstroke.

Downcurve; undercurve.

Downcurve; undercurve.
Slant; loop forward.
Undercurve.

Cursive Stroke Descriptions

● Overcurve; slant.
Overcurve; slant; undercurve.

Overcurve; slant.
Overcurve; slant.
Overcurve; slant; undercurve.

Overcurve; slant; undercurve.
Slant; loop back; overcurve.

Overcurve; slant; undercurve (lift).
Slant.

Overcurve; slant; undercurve.
Checkstroke.

● Overcurve; slant.
Overcurve; curve down; loop; overcurve.

Downcurve; undercurve.
Slant; undercurve.

Downcurve; undercurve; loop; curve right.

Downcurve; loop; curve down and up; loop; curve right.

Slant.
Downcurve; undercurve.

● Slant.
Downcurve; loop; downcurve; undercurve.

Curve forward; slant.
Overcurve; slant; undercurve.

Curve forward; slant.
Overcurve; slant.
Overcurve; slant; undercurve.

Curve forward; slant (lift).
Curve back; slant.
Retrace; loop; curve right.

Curve forward; slant (lift).
Doublecurve.
Curve forward and down; undercurve.

Curve forward; slant; undercurve.
Slant; undercurve.

Curve forward; slant; undercurve.
Slant; loop back; overcurve.

Curve forward and down; slant. Overcurve; curve down; loop; overcurve.

Curve forward; slant; undercurve; overcurve.

Curve forward; slant; undercurve.
Slant; undercurve; overcurve.

Curve forward; slant; undercurve (lift).
Slant.

Cursive Stroke Descriptions

Overcurve; curve down and up.
Retrace; curve right.

Overcurve; slant; loop back;
overcurve.

Curve back; overcurve; curve
down; retrace; curve forward;
curve under.

Slant.
Curve forward and right (lift).
Doublecurve; curve up.
Retrace; curve right.

Slant.
Curve forward and right (lift).
Doublecurve; curve up.
Retrace; curve right (lift).
Slide right.

Undercurve; loop; curve forward.
Doublecurve; curve up.
Retrace; curve right.

Undercurve; loop; curve down
and up.
Retrace; curve right.

Undercurve; loop; curve down;
loop; curve under.

Undercurve.
Slant.
Retrace; curve forward and
back.

Undercurve.
Slant.
Retrace; curve forward and back.
Curve forward; undercurve.

Undercurve.
Slant.
Retrace; curve forward; loop;
curve forward and back.
Retrace; curve right.

Slant.

Slant.
Curve forward; slant.
Curve right.

Slant.
Curve forward and back.
Curve forward and back.

Slant.
Slide right (lift).
Slant.

Slant.
Curve forward and back (lift).
Slide right.

Curve down and forward;
loop.

Slant.
Doublecurve.
Slant.

Curve back and down; curve
back; slant up.

Downcurve; undercurve.
Slant.

Slant (lift).
Downcurve; undercurve.

Name: _____

● Complete the information form for the yearbook. Use your best manuscript writing.

Name: _____

Nickname: _____

Grade: _____

Teacher: _____

Activities: _____

● Hobbies: _____

Favorite class: _____

Least favorite lunch item: _____

Summer plans: _____

Goals for next year: _____

_____

●

Practice Master 61